INSTANT RESULTS

3 Proven Steps To Make Your Dreams Come True

Be BRAVE

Be DIFFERENT

Be YOU

Livia Liyanto

ISBN 978-94-92827-00-5

This book is dedicated to YOU.

I am opening my life story to inspire and empower you. This is my way of passing it forward.

Would you kindly pass this book to someone else who can be inspired by my story and as a means for you to help them?

Love,
LL

Connect with me by scanning this code:

TABLE OF CONTENT

FOREWORD

I first knew Livia when she was shy! She is still a shy person; you see how she has overcome her shyness when you identify in her writings the power she has within her.

As a mentor I shift woman's idea to a new reality finding their why and empowering their time, their style, their confidence and their profit to a global She'preneur status.

I relate to Livia's story in many ways, she has been driven by why she has survived and now she is self-directed while she thrives as a wife, a lover and a mother, giving her story more than depth, it's real. Her story is from her experience.

Livia had a dream, each time she saw a step towards that dream, she took each step with effective actions.

I admire her courageousness, she stepped out of her comfort zone to grow herself.

She found her inner voice and now is able to facilitate other voices – globally, through her book and presentations for the betterment of our planet.

This story demonstrates how a young woman can be a role model before having a clue of what true responsibilities are. Livia simply knew what she couldn't see, feel or touch was her reality. Her journey has come from inside herself, not from a text book or some guru's words of wisdom.

Livia Liyanto's life story, through this book, will empower YOU to pursue your dreams and beyond. Her proven system will not only save you time, but also will empower you to attract money and the life you may never dreamt of having.

Read every word you will be shocked by her personal transformation along with her empowering story!

I believe this is truly her gift to you. I hope you will take action after reading this book by taking the control of your own life, be the boss of your life.

Best Selling Author, International Speaker, Mentor - Di Downie

PROLOGUE

Imagine waking up in the morning, feeling excited because today, just as every single day, you wake up knowing that it will be exactly the day you have been imagined. Wake up with a sense of purpose. Having the clarity of what you want to pursue and achieve. All your relationships are loving. You have enough money to do everything you want. You are also monetizing your goals and dreams and doing what you love to do. You help people to become more successful. You feel absolutely fulfilled. No more self-limitation and nothing to hold back. No more compromise. No need to hide, because you realize that you and your experiences are important. Finally, you are free and independent. You found your true power.

Your life is transformed, from average to amazing.

What if, every day you have the opportunity that you have been looking for?

You now give permission to design the life you were meant to live, based on your dreams and passions.

You now live life by your own design and you celebrate every single day.

Many people know that I am shy and introvert person but I would like to gift my story to you because I believe my story will inspire and empower you to move forward. I would love to see your transformation.

Deep down inside, you know what you love to do. Get ready for some soul-searching.

CHAPTER 1 - How It All Started

"Don't dream too high.

If you fall, you will get hurt."

I have the deepest love imaginable for my paternal grandparents who took care of me from the time I was a little girl. They were full of warmth and kindness and all things beautiful and amazing. I loved them so much. I spent most of my pre-elementary school years in their home and enjoyed every bit of time I spent with them, including picking fresh, sweet *srikaya* (custard apple) straight from their tree.

I grew up in the town of Pekalongan, in central Java, Indonesia. It was and is a small town well-known for its batik—an amazing technique of wax-resistant dyeing which was applied to fabrics.

When it was time to go to elementary school, I returned to my parents' house. But to this day my grandparents' house still holds many beautiful memories. It was always "homey." My grandmother was a passionate mother and grandmother who loved to cook. The delicious aroma of something cooking on the kitchen stove would fill her entire house. Her home-cooked meals ensured her children and grandchildren kept visiting. It was the most delicious food I've ever tasted!

My paternal grandparents had been Chinese immigrants. As a child, I remember watching my grandfather struggling to eat with a spoon and fork because he had only ever eaten with chopsticks before. There was Chinese on my mother's side too, but my mother's great-grandparents had been born in Indonesia.

My grandfather ran a successful tofu company which he had founded several years previously and managed by himself. I just loved visiting the factory as a child. Grandma would often cook mouth-watering meals which she would bring it Grandpa's factory for all the employees. She made the best soy milk in the world! Oh how I miss that taste so much!

Grandma often took me to a *klenteng* temple where she was an active member. She loved meeting people there and cooking for them. The temple exists to this day, and although I have a different religion today, the temple will be always a part of me, a constant reminder of my childhood with my grandparents. Everyone in the *klenteng* knew I their little girl. As a matter of fact, everyone in Pekalongan knew it. In our town, almost everybody knew one another. Moreover, my grandparents were well-known people within the Indonesian-Chinese community.

My maternal grandparents were also well known because of their business. They owned a franchise company which they ran for almost forty years. They were excellent at customer service, and as a result had many loyal clients. One valuable lesson my grandmother taught me was this: If you take care of your customers with love and dedication, they will always come back.

My parents had a business too, as did my uncles on both sides. It's safe to say that I come from a family of entrepreneurs.

Movies were a significant part of my childhood. I will remember two favourite movies for as long as I live. My mother said I loved to watch them over and over again. In fact, I was practically addicted to them.

One was Candy-Candy, a romantic Japanese *manga*. So you can guess that I am a hopeless romantic. I daydreamed a lot, hoping so much that one day I would have my own romantic story. The second movie was Goggle V, the Japanese version of *Power Rangers*. When I saw that movie as a small child, I spoke no Japanese at all. But I watched it so often that now, almost thirty years later, the song and the text are still vivid in my mind. Bizarrely, I can still sing the opening song of Goggle V!

I loved to read, too. I was the only one in the family who did, and my mother appreciated it. So she often bought me imported "luxury" books such as encyclopaedias and good night story books from Hans Christian Andersen. I was so proud of my book collection, and no wonder, because they were all expensive books that were hard to come by.

I had a memorable childhood, being pampered by both grandparents in terms of money and love. For my birthday every year they threw a big party for me, which I didn't mind at all! All that mattered to me were the gifts I received on each occasion. Barbie dolls and book were my only interests.

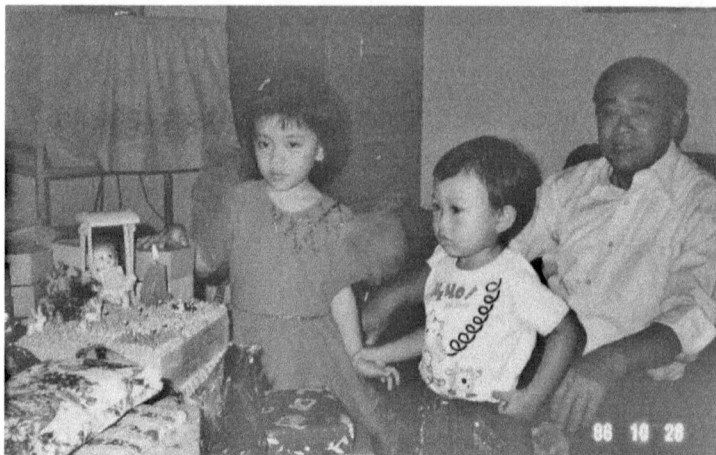

I remember I had always the best snack in the class, came fresh right away from the bakery and there was another girl in the class who took my snack almost every day and I could not fight for myself. I got angry or cry at home. I did not fight something I deserve. I was weak. That was all. I could not complain for the rests.

If I could turn back the clock, I would love to go back to that place and time—the town of my birth and of my amazing childhood. Too bad my grandparents died before I could make them proud of me. Every time I think of them, I regret I never managed to do anything extraordinary while they were alive. I was just a simple young girl with no special abilities.

In elementary school, I was a good "average" pupil. I was not the prettiest girl in the class, nor the richest. In regard to academic achievement, I was never first in the class. Normally I was about third. I may have been better than most other students, but I was still not at the top.

I had a few good friends. Monika, Susana and Jun are the ones that readily come to mind now. After school we played a lot together, mostly at Jun's house because it was the most fun. His room was filled with a huge number of toys of all kinds, and they were all fun to play with. His mother would give us snacks to take home. One of them—my favourite—was the Ceres chocolate sprinkles.

If my grandparents were well-off, my parents were too. My father owned a car business and my mother had a popular book store in the city. Sometimes I went to my parents' house, and as I got older, my visits became more frequent. I had two maids to take care of me. *Why two?* you might ask. First of all, my parents were busy. But it was quite normal to have full-time house assistant(s) in Indonesia, especially when you were rich.

I began to develop my business skills while still in elementary school. I remember obtaining a lot of stuff from my mother's store and asking my team (my nephew and my brother) to sell it for me. Basically, I got the items from my mother for free. Then I charged my team members $1 per piece, for example. Since it was so long ago I can't recall the exact price. I told them to mark up the items to whatever price they wanted, say $3 each. From memory, our book covers were the best sellers. I had different types of cute covers that made the books less boring and more appealing.

I motivated my team to make money! As I look back, I am amazed I could do this at such a young age. I taught my team how to sell. It was a win-win situation and we all made a lot of money, especially my nephew who was very amenable to my coaching and followed my advice to the letter. He sold more than my brother who was less teachable at the time but came up with plenty of excuses for not selling.

Don't expect result from excuses!

When I got into junior high school, I parted ways with most of my elementary school friends, since most of them went on to private schools. This was normal in our city. Normally, Indonesian-Chinese people such as myself would go to a private school.

Some people felt you were not a local if you had different "blood." By contrast, in the Netherlands, if you are born locally then you are considered a local. Although I, my parents and my maternal grandparents had been born in Indonesia, some people still described me as 'Chinese' because of my Chinese blood.

I was proud of my Indonesian heritage and would often tell people I was a local Indonesian, although some "real" Indonesian people didn't always appreciate that (PS. What is "real" anyway?). This is why the Indonesian-Chinese kids usually went to private schools, while the "real" locals went to public schools. The other common opinion was that if you had Chinese blood but went to a public school, which was much cheaper, then you must be poor.

In the small town in which I grew up, everyone was privy to everyone else's decisions. As such, we all ended up valuing other people's opinions and living for their approval. I used to live this way. I'd listen to and be influenced by the opinions of others. Whether or not they were correct didn't matter. We had to at least try to understand what others would be thinking about us. And if we made unfortunate mistakes, they would always stay in the community like an old wine stain that could never be washed away. Mistakes were a constant source of shame to a big family, and nobody wanted them to happen.

As a local, I went into the top public junior high school in Pekalongan, SMPN 1. Nobody forced me to go there, but I chose to go. I wanted to burst out of the bubble that my friends from elementary school were in. I did not want to be restricted to a private school that was filled with rich people of influence. I was happy to interact with friends from different races and religions and I learned a lot from them. Despite being in the minority, I played with everyone because I didn't see any differences. As long as they were good people, I wanted to be friends with them. For me, race and religion were just the clothes they wore, and I still believe this.

I knew about religions, at least superficially, having come from a multi-religious family and environment. My family members included Buddhists, Muslims and Christians. When I was in junior high school, my mother asked me to join her in Catholic instruction classes. As a "good girl," I had accompanied her and followed her advice. I became a practising Catholic, although I had no deep relationship with God at that time. Only after I was at university, and living alone, did I choose the Catholic faith for myself. I still visited different churches and temples, accompanied by friends, but I had already made my choice. Having a personal relationship with God gave me a new sense of peace.

As time went on, life seemed to grow more serious. I began to hear of depressing news, such as the bankruptcy of my paternal grandfather. My grandparents began to stay at home more often and the tofu company was shut down. I still visited them almost every day. Sometimes I asked them and my other family members for more information but I always got the same answer: "You are still young; don't concern yourself with adults' problems." So I never knew exactly what happened, and my grandparents did their best not to be sad in front of me. I almost never saw them angry, either. Sometimes I would see a shadow of pain pass over my grandfather's face when he thought no one was looking but it disappeared as soon as he realized I was staring at him.

It was the same thing with my parents. When the book store was closed, we moved to a housing area in a quieter place. I never knew why it was closed. I felt bad about that because apart from the fact that I liked being at the store, it always seemed busy with customers and business certainly looked good. Again, as a child I was not allowed to ask any questions.

Much later, I found out what had caused my grandparents' bankruptcy and set my family's finances on a downward spiral. My grandfather's second in command, whom he had trusted so much, had betrayed him. He had taken over the firm and left my grandfather with nothing. Grandfather even had to pay a lot of money to wind up the company, including compensation for all the employees. Worse still, Grandfather eventually lost the ownership of his own land. How could somebody we had helped, somebody we had trusted, stab us in the back and take everything we had? How could anyone be so heartless? I could not understand it.

Despite all that happened, however, my grandparents remained positive. They didn't say one bad thing about the turn of events and the man who had fleeced them, even though I insisted on knowing and helping. Angry, hurt and sad, I wished I could do something. I appreciated their positive attitude but they really didn't deserve this.

Meanwhile I was happy in our new house and neighbourhood, and acquired more friends of around my age. This was before the era of technology, and we played outside every day. Several games kept us busy. Sometimes we played hide and seek and sometimes we just chatted on the bench outside the house. Three of my neighbours, Icha, Emma and Ivan, were also my friends at school.

I had more activities in school now, and they kept me busy. It was cool to be in junior high school at last. At first my mother still took me to school, but soon our lovely neighbour took me to school every day, together with Ivan, his son. Ivan was a morning person but I most definitely was not. I woke up pretty late every single day and Ivan got frustrated at having to wait for me. His parents were good people, though, and always welcomed me. After school I would go home with some of my friends, using public transportation such as a small bus or a *becak* (tricycle).

My academic achievement was still good, and I was among the top ten percent of the class. (Each class had +-45 children but that was normal). However, my English still needed work. I had been studying English for several years in school with little progress because I did not practise outside of school. My first language is Javanese and second Indonesian. I spoke Mandarin when I was small while living with my grandparents. I was used to hearing several languages since my grandpa spoke Mandarin, Hokkien and other Chinese dialects. I watched Japanese movies before I watched Western Movies. Goggle V existed before Power Rangers. As time passed, I would watch Western movies but read the subtitles. Hence, the reason why I could not master one language fluently because I had too many influences growing up! I will never forget being bullied in High School because my English was not good and was teased for the sound of my voice. So growing up I have been shy and introverted most of my life. Back then, I guess it made me believe that I would never have a voice let alone being a public speaker... Also growing up you realize that true friends would never make fun of you or make you feel bad, would they?

About this time an American boy band called the Backstreet Boys were famous. The first time I saw one of the members, Nick Carter, I fell in love with him. For me, this was absolute and irrevocable. It was not just love; I also became his greatest fan. I started to dream, and this time it was big! I told my friends Nick was my boyfriend. I cut his pictures from magazines and pasted them on my wallet and all my books. I told my grandma about this too, because I was comfortable telling her most things. She taught me something I will always remember:

"Don't dream high, please, my love! If you fall, you will hurt a lot."

I laughed every time she said this because I knew I was going to get in touch with Nick Carter someday and marry him. It was an unshakable conviction, although I didn't yet know how I would go about it.

I was almost at the end of my third year in junior high school when my maternal grandma told me something that made me ecstatic, something I could only have dreamed of. One of her sisters lived in New Zealand and she told my grandma that she could probably sponsor me so I could live there and attend a senior high school. I was over the moon, as it would bring me one step closer to Nick Carter. He lived in USA and I would live in New Zealand. The only question was "How would I connect with him?"

My hopes were dashed a couple of weeks later when I was told I wouldn't be traveling to New Zealand after all. My family offered me a couple reasons that I did not understand. They tried to explain a lot of things, but I was never sure what the real reason was. I tried hard not to be disappointed. Life had to go on.

My uncle and aunt who lived in Semarang, the capital city of Central Java, suggested I apply to the best private senior high school in Semarang, Loyola college. So I did this, as well as applying to the best senior high school in Pekalongan.

I then spent three months' holiday in Semarang for two reasons. First, I wanted to apply for Loyola College, and secondly, I wanted to learn English. During my holiday, I did a summer course in the best English institution in Semarang. Its teachers were native English speakers and it was much more expensive than the usual English course, but I was determined to learn there.

My uncle told me I was not fortunate enough to get accepted at Loyola College. We were not willing to pay extra money as a school donation, and my academic achievement was probably not good enough either. However, all this was fine by me. I'd had a wonderful time learning English and befriended my twenty-one-year-old teacher. She was from Canada and her name was Hailey. She would regale me with stories about her homeland, which I loved to hear.

She also came out to Pekalongan one weekend, to find out what my hometown was like. People loved to stare at her. I guess this was understandable since Pekalongan was a small city and not the usual destination of international tourists. So foreign tourists were rare, and they became instant celebrities. People loved to have their pictures taken with them as it made them feel important.

After Semarang, I went back to Pekalongan but put less energy into academic work. My parents had pinned their hopes on me. They wanted me to achieve academically because they knew I could do it. But I still did not know what I wanted to do with my life. Hence, I had no reason or motivation to work hard. I just wanted to enjoy my life. I was still in the top ten percent, but I could have done better. I preferred to sit at the back of my classroom, chatting with friends while the teachers were teaching. I saw no reason to learn all the details of physics and mathematics. All these formulas and whatnot seemed tedious and unimportant. *Would I ever need these in real life?* I wondered. Nor did my English improve. Some of my friends laughed when they heard me trying to speak it. This depressed me and I began to wonder if I even had the talent to speak English.

Deep inside my heart, however, the desire to go abroad and meet Nick Carter still burned brightly! But I had still had no idea how it was going to happen.

Towards the end of my time as a high school student, I heard many people talking about their desire to go on to university. They had picked their direction and their university. I had not. A single question gnawed at me, "What is my strength?", "What do I want in life?", "What do I want to become?"

Some of my friends went to universities abroad. Oh, how lucky they were! I wished I had a super-rich family. Having seen student life in many movies, I would love to have known what it was like to go to college and university in another country.

After a while, I was forced to contemplate what I wanted in life. Having an intense desire to study something which could bring me closer to my dream in an international environment, I finally decided to take a course called International Relations.

"What on earth is *that*?" asked my family members and some other friends.

"It's part of the faculty of political science. We'll learn all about international matters."

"And what kind of work would that lead to?"

"Anything connected to international companies, I guess."

Frankly, I wasn't sure. It wasn't a popular course of study in our town. People normally took courses such as chemical or mechanical engineering, architecture, management or economics. For older people in Pekalongan, other disciplines such as international relations or languages and literature weren't known at all.

As time passed, I grew to not care what people thought of my choice. I had decided firmly on my direction, and that was it. I chose to do International Relations at the Parahyangan Catholic University, which happened to offer the best course in the country on this subject. Not only that, but it was the best private university in Indonesia, and at that time International Relations was its most popular major.

I was satisfied with my choice, but my mother still tried make me change my mind.

"How about studying medicine?" she asked. "You could do your masters in cosmetology after that and make a lot of money!"

Indonesian parents generally saw medicine and law as lucrative professions. But medicine was not for me, especially as I despised the sight of my own blood.

A possible second choice (my family advised me to have one "just in case") was to study psychology at Maranatha Christian University. But I already knew what I wanted and felt strongly that I would get it.

My lovely grandparents were worried. They asked me to study in Semarang rather than Bandung because Semarang was just two hours from Pekalongan, while Bandung was a nine-hour drive away.

"If anything ever happened," my grandmother told me, "we could quickly be there to help you."

They also felt happier about Semarang since my uncle and aunt lived there. But I was adamant. Bandung it had to be.

CHAPTER 2 - Know What You Want

"Dreams come true... If you have one."

So, you need to KNOW WHAT YOU WANT and have the COURAGE to go for it!

In the past, my grandma, my family and even later on the family of my ex-boyfriend called me a dreamer. Despite being bullied for my voice and my lack of fluency in English speaking, I realized that I am a dreamer and plan on accomplishing everything I have ever dreamt about.

Being a big dreamer doesn't mean that you have to walk around with your head in the clouds. It simply means that you're seeking a purpose for your life and it means that you're becoming fulfilled in the process.

Doesn't matter how old you are, it's not late for you to start!

Having had big dreams drove me to the point where I stand today. Unfortunately, many of you scared to think big, to have a big dream. Why? Because your parents or your environment will tell you that you are crazy?

A dream is an inspiring picture of the future that energizes you mind and your emotions. A dream will empower you to do everything you can to achieve it!

Dreaming involves holding tight to a vision of a better life, one of success and abundance. Realize that there's a long road ahead and your big dreams won't come easy. Otherwise, they wouldn't be worthwhile. If everyone could do it, then what would be the challenge in it?

So many people spend their life without any idea of what they want. People work so hard to make money and then they try to buy "happiness" (vacation, cars, houses, luxury goods). As a result, they've become slaves to their own life.

Here are the reasons why some of you have trouble identifying your dreams:

1.   Lack of imagination. So start imagining!
2.   Discouragement by others. Remember that my grandma told me not to dream high? I love her so much with all my heart and soul but luckily I did not listen to her in this case.
3.   Lack of courage to pursue your dreams. The role of mentor and coach are very crucial here, they are the most important people in your life who will lead and guide you to make your dreams come true.
4.   Have habit of settling for average.
The minute you settle for less than you deserve, you get even less than you settled for. You cannot reach for

dream and remain safely mediocre at the same time. Be brave, get out of your comfort zone!

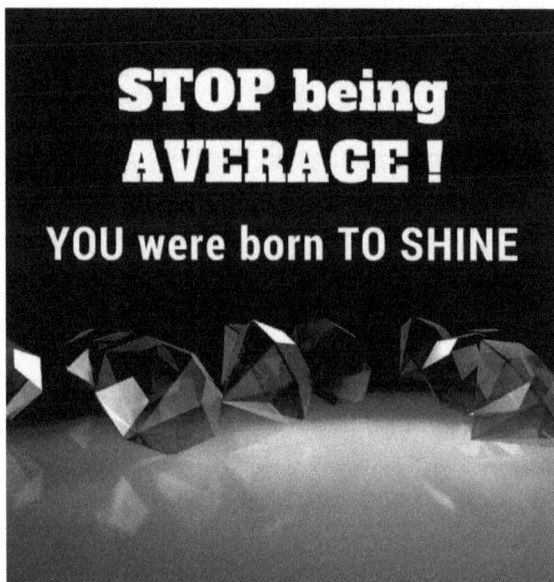

How much does it cost to think and dream big? Nothing!

It is FREE to think, so think big, dream big and make it happen!!!

I did not let someone who saw me as a joke define my future. In fact, I am now an international speaker who inspire and empower others to take ownership of their own life. Could you imagine if I had listened to him in the past?

Take the time carefully analyse where you are now and what you want to accomplish in your life. Then start to set goals to help you accomplish your objectives. If you don't know where you want to go, you will have no idea of what to do in order to get there.

> *GPS works best if you know where you want to go (your destination).*

I have a good example. I remember a few months ago, I drove from Haarlem to Hoofddorp and I had an intention to stop by at a specific grocery store. I did not use my GPS because I thought I knew the way in Hoofddorp. After arriving at the store, I realized that if I had used my GPS since I started in Haarlem, I would have saved my time and money because the GPS would calculate and lead me to the shortest and quickest route from Haarlem to the store.

By not using my GPS, it cost me time and money.

In life, you may think you are saving money by not having mentors and coaches but would actually it cost you money by not having mentors and coaches to guide you in life.

Now let's go back to set goals to help you accomplish your objectives.

Meaningful goals are an essential requirement for success in business. With goals, you have a target to aim for, a purpose for being, and a direction to travel. Without goals, it's easy to wander aimlessly, getting side tracked with any little thing that comes along.

When you set your goals, think of the word, "SMART." You should have SMART goals. That is, your goals should be:

1. Specific - Consider who, what, when, where, why and how in developing the goal.

2. Measurable - Include a numeric or descriptive measurement.

3. Achievable - Consider the resources needed and set a realistic goal.

4. Realistic - Make sure the goal is consistent with the mission be realistic in your expectations compare to the timing and efforts.

5. Time-bound - Set a realistic deadline.

The only thing holding you back from achieving them, is yourself. Thoughts are things. What you think, you become. If you think you can, you can! If you think you can't, you can't!

It is that simple.

Great things CAN and WILL HAPPEN to you if you can just find the courage to pursue them and do whatever it takes. You will achieve great things and you may even end up achieving more than you ever thought you could.

If Columbus, Thomas Alva Edison and Oprah didn't dream big, what would have happened?

Oh wait,

What if our children were Christopher Columbus, Thomas Alva Edison, Oprah, Steve Jobs or Mark Zuckerberg?

Children dream big. They never think small because they aren't hindered by the standard limitations that hold adults back. Unlike adults, children's dreams have no ceiling.

It's easy to dismiss a child's dreams as being silly or unrealistic but who's to say any of our dreams are silly or unrealistic? How could you judge the future? So when you read this, please promise me that you will not dismiss your children's dreams. Instead you will support them to pursue their dreams. Don't let our society or negative environment stop our children's dreams. Your child could be the future's president or someone who has the ability to change people's life! You should believe in your children, why? Because they believe in themselves. If you are on their side, anything is possible.

For our children, we are their inspiration, motivator and leader.

In case you are a parent, I have some tips to help our children's dream into reality:

- Don't deny their dreams
- Don't control their dreams
- Be a good example for your children
- Help them to develop the plan and to execute
- Show your support

"If your dreams don't scare you, then they're not big enough."

BE BRAVE! Dare to dream!

CHAPTER 3 - Connect The Dots

"If you are soft on yourself, life will be hard for you.

If you are hard on yourself, life will be soft for you"

After I moved to Bandung, connections my friendships with people from Pekalongan continued for a few months, but they weren't to last. Within six months I'd made good friends among non-Pekalongan people, including most of the young students who lived next door.

I was living in a girls' hostel, next door to a hostel for male students. Often I visited them just to chat, and sometimes I'd eat lunch with one of them. I felt quite safe with these guys, who treated me like a sister. There was only one who annoyed me a little.

On campus, I struggled to wake up early, especially for the economics class which always started by 8 a.m. Sometimes I saw my male class mates coming to the class in slippers. Evidently, I was not the only one who had difficulty waking early!

To fill in my free time, I volunteered to help on the events committee of the Political Science faculty. I felt this would provide good experiences and friendships, and who knew whether it might lead to some job opportunity overseas?

It was about this time that people of my generation were beginning to use the internet, and I was soon hooked. I loved spending time on the internet, chatting with friends who were living abroad. One of my friends, Teddy, was from Pekalongan but he'd lived in Los Angeles for a long time. I loved hearing his story and hoped that someday I too would have the chance to go to the USA.

Because I went to one internet café regularly, and perhaps because the owners saw me as reliable, I was offered work as the cafe manager and put in charge of managing the finances. The owners, two young men from Medan, were kind to me and treated me like one of the family, but frankly, I took the job only because it gave me free internet access. The money was just a bonus, as it always was when I did things I liked doing.

All in all, I enjoyed my time at the Parahyangan Catholic University (UNPAR). I had many friends of different ethnicities, religions and cultures, and I learned how to interact well with them all. Ike, my best friend, was a Javanese from Jakarta, and it was Ike with whom I shared my private life. We studied together and spent a lot of time on and off the campus. Ike knew everything about me, including the fact that although I had a boyfriend, my goal was to marry Nick Carter.

Then there was Jimmy, who, like me, was from Central Java. He graduated from Loyola College High School, the school I had not been accepted for. Jimmy was my best friend through thick and thin, regardless of who my current boyfriend was. He was also crazy about Japan and Korea.

It was from Jimmy that I obtained my antique-collection of childhood favourites, Goggle V. By this time my enthusiasm for western countries had begun to fade and I was switching my focus to countries such as Japan and Korea. My goals changed too. Now my dream was to marry a handsome man from Japan or Korea—preferably a super romantic one! I even took a Japanese language course for extra study and passed the equivalency test in Japanese. Korean dramas and movies were starting to boom and I was soon addicted to them, despite the fact that all the plots were basically the same: a young handsome, rich and romantic Korean man would fall in love with an ordinary girl.

I was living in a beautiful fantasy world, and decided I would marry Jo In Sung or Rain (they are Korean actor/singer) instead of Nick Carter. I even wrote a few novels based on my fantasies.

Mine was pretty much a normal student's life, however. It consisted of study, fun, shopping, girl time, volunteering, relationships, reading and writing. I would write at every opportunity. It beat doing nothing!

I was introduced by one of my friends, a smart young woman called Juliana, to her business. She also introduced me to her mentor, Joko, who became was my first business mentor. Always positive and helpful, he took time to listen to my business and non-business concerns. This kindled my interest in business and I began to read motivational books on the subject. (One of them was the famous *Rich Dad, Poor Dad*). I also attended several seminars on business and related affairs. I learned about the "Cash Flow Quadrant." People on the right side of the quadrant valued freedom and financial liberty and didn't relish working for the rest of their lives as employees. I wanted to be in this right quadrant as an investor.

At one business event I met an older man and we talked for a while. He told me he liked me very much and wanted me to meet his nephew.

"He's a good man and he's still single," he said, "If you don't mind, I'd like to introduce you to him."

I didn't mind. That was how I met Fendy. He had no money when we met, and we were good friends for a year before he asked me to be his girlfriend. All he owned was an old motorcycle, but he was committed to starting a business. Every evening after he was through with his work, he would work on the business and I would help him with it.

In six years, I learned a lot from him. I learned about leadership and team building. I learned how to handle diversity and objections. He taught me about building a business, creating a passive income, and staying humble. Our business grew slowly in the beginning but by the end of the second year we had made a lot of money and continued to do so. Soon we had various luxury properties and luxury cars, but we continued to work hard to reach even greater goals.

Fendy taught me something I would never forget:

If you are soft on yourself, life will be hard for you, but if you are hard on yourself, life will be soft for you.

I went back to Pekalongan twice each year to visit my family and spend time them. I always made time for my grandparents. Their eyes lit up whenever they saw me. I would always be their little girl, and a source of joy for them. As I write this, my tears are flowing. I still miss them so much.

Sometimes I would accompany my grandmother to buy groceries at the local market. On one occasion she wanted to buy something nice for her other grandchildren, but was hesitant. I was sure it was because she had limited money and needed to spend her money wisely. I had some money and could easily have bought it but she always refused to let me.

"You must keep it for yourself," she said. "Save it for a rainy day."

When I demurred, she became even more insistent.

Sometimes she asked me, as people did in Indonesia, when I was going to tie the knot. This was when I had only been at university for a couple of years.

"We want our granddaughter to be married," she said.

I was sorry that I could not please her happy in this matter, but I was just not ready for marriage.

Meanwhile I finished my bachelor's degree in International Relations. I didn't plan to work for money because our business was already running smoothly, so I volunteered to teach in an elementary public school in Bandung. Life was busy with all my activities and the business.

Soon after I graduated, my grandma fell ill. When I went to visit, her the topic of marriage came up again. She said she would love to see me married before she "departed." Since Jakarta, being the capital city, had more modern facilities, Grandmother was admitted to a city hospital, where she stayed for months. I visited her often and sometimes I would stay in Jakarta for couple days just so I could spend time with my grandparents. My grandfather never left her side. He moved into the hospital too, and stayed there.

One sunny afternoon I accompanied my grandfather to a supermarket to buy food. On our way back he saw a nice bag in a shop window. He waited in front of the store and stared at the bag for a while. Then he decided to buy it for my grandmother. After he saw the price, however, he changed his mind.

I insisted on buying it—after all, I could afford it—but my grandfather wouldn't have a bar of that. I knew I could buy that bag easily but Grandfather put his food down. He told me he would be angry if I bought that bag.

"Keep your money for yourself!" he said.

My heart still hurts.

Grandmother passed away after staying in the hospital for a couple of months. It was one of the saddest moments of my life. I cried for several days, and even months later, tears would well up. She had been my friend as well as my grandmother. She had always been there for me and I loved her so much. I regretted I had not been able to fulfil her heart's desire by marrying the boyfriend whom I had been seeing for six years now.

Why was I waiting? Did I want to get married? Why did I keep putting it off? Questions like these swirled in my head. Fendy was everything a girl and her parents could dream of. He was honest, hardworking, trustworthy, kind, patient and calm. He was also making good money. He had all the right qualities!

For the past four years, my family, friends, relatives and even strangers had been asking us when we were going to get married. Like any Indonesian woman, I wanted to get married and have children at a young age. Yet something inside prevented me from taking that step. I couldn't explain the reason, but my heart just wasn't ready.

You said you wanted to travel around the world? my heart whispered to me. *You want to live in another country, feel the snow, and experience other countries and cultures? You want to be alone and feel how strong you are? You want the freedom to hold opinions and to chart your own course?*

I want to! my brain answered. *But how?*

I had wanted these things all my life. At first, I'd thought it was just a childish whim that would disappear with time, but I soon realized it was more than that. The drive was so strong and insistent, and no matter how hard I tried, I could not ignore it.

I had struggled with these thoughts for a long time. They had not suddenly surfaced after six years of friendship with Fendy. As a matter of fact, I'd been having them since the fourth year of our relationship. Back then I'd already been asking myself, *Is this what I really want?*

Obviously, with our financial situation I could have travelled abroad whenever and wherever I wanted. I had been living comfortably with luxury cars and a luxury home. We were building a big villa too. I could get married and have children while I was still quite young. Many people envied my comfortable position. Why would I throw it all away? Nor did I want to feel that the six years I had spent with Fendy were wasted. Did I really want to ditch this luxurious life to start over? I'd be *crazy* to do so!

My brain worked hard to mute the callings of my heart. My heart yearned for freedom, while my head told me to be reasonable. I explored every ramification of each choice, and finally reached my decision. I wanted to travel abroad. To do this I had two options, to work or to study. Working abroad was less of a possibility now, since I'd had little experience with international companies. So I skipped this option. That left the alternative of studying abroad. So I started to do TOEFL and IELTS courses to improve my English.

Meanwhile I researched the possibilities of completing a master's degree at one of the European universities. Finally, instead of applying to five or six universities, as other people had advised me to do, I ended up applying to just one university in Norway. I knew this limited my chances of going abroad, but I did have a good feeling about this particular university. I also figured that since my chances of getting in were minimal, if I did make it through it would mean that God had helped me. I concluded this because every day I asked God to guide me. If I didn't get accepted by that university, it would mean staying with Fendy for the rest of my life.

I opted to follow my heart and leave my comfort zone. My family questioned my crazy decision and still hoped I would eventually change my mind.

My grandfather's health declined progressively, despite all that the family did to keep him well. I guess he was just too lonely after Grandma's passing. Whenever and wherever he met people, he would always tell them how great Grandma had been. He told them she was the best woman he had ever known. What could I do? I had no idea how to make him feel better. So I called him frequently, to keep his mind off his loss.

Then I got some good news: I had been accepted into the Master's program in Norway! I considered this to be a sign from God, and decided to break up with my boyfriend. Everyone protested. They couldn't believe I really wanted to follow this path, and didn't want me to take a step I might one-day regret. I totally understood how they felt. Why become poor if you have a lot of money? (I would become poor because I didn't want to take a cent of the money I had earned with my ex-boyfriend. I felt guilty enough about my decision to leave him.)

Studying in another country was the only way I achieve my dream to live abroad. For Asian people, especially Indonesians, it was almost impossible to travel and live abroad if you didn't have financial help from your family. The only exceptions were those students in the top ten percent who received scholarships, as I did.

All my friends from Pekalongan went to universities abroad because they had financial support from their parents. So how could I survive abroad without any money? I didn't yet know, but I wasn't worried. How I would get money was a secondary concern. The main thing was that I wanted to travel. It was the only way I could prove to myself that I was strong enough to survive alone in a foreign country.

Your why is more important than your how!

A master's degree was not my goal. I wanted to learn about life and dig deeper into myself. With my comfortable life back in Indonesia, I had limited opportunities to learn about life in the wider world, for almost all my decisions were influenced by family, neighbours and culture. To make this huge choice by myself made me feel powerful. I was not a product of circumstances; I was a product of my own decisions.

I'd spent most of my life taking care of everyone around me and living by someone else's rules. I'd been the "good girl" for years, but never felt fulfilled. The pressures took a major toll on my health, my relationships, my jobs and my confidence. All this continued until I learned to break the pattern. I decided time to nurture myself and pursue my passions. I broke free to do all I wanted to do, whether this was to travel the world, go back to school, or build my career. It was I who made the decision to start over, to do something different. The real me needed to come alive.

If I could do it, anyone could!

We can never anticipate how God will intervene in our lives. I had prepared everything for my departure, and four weeks before I was to leave, I met with a friend of my friend, Linda. She had lived in the Netherlands for a year as an *au pair* and she was enjoying her vacation time in Bandung before leaving again for Belgium to be an *au pair* again. When she explained her job to me, a bell suddenly rang my brain. *This was it!* What an opportunity to travel, work and study!

The night after I met Linda, I asked God, *Father, is this the way You have provided for me?*

There was no answer, so I re-phrased my question: *Father, if this is the way You have provided for me, please let me get a host family within a month. If I don't, then I'll take it that I am to continue with the original plan.*

I fell asleep soon after saying that prayer. I was supposed to depart for Norway the following month. In three months' time, I would be 26 years old, which was the maximum age to be an *au pair* in the Netherlands.

I had made enquiries to an *au pair* agency and been told it would normally take three months to get a host family. They told me there were times when families needed more time to get to know the proposed *au pair*. If they didn't have a good feeling about you, then you had to wait for a new family. They told me anything could come up to prevent an au pair from getting a host family quickly. So I set a one-month time limit, knowing that if I got a host family within that time, it meant that the Lord was leading me.

Fortunately, it turned out to be God's way. Within two weeks I was contacted by a host family who had a five-month-old baby. I couldn't help wondering how I was going to take care of it. I wasn't experienced with babies, but this family felt I was the right choice.

To cut a long story short, I was accepted by the family who took care of the necessary paperwork so I could depart the following month. I contacted the people at the university and cancelled my course. I felt excited about this new opportunity.

Unfortunately, my family, especially my aunts, were not at all impressed.

"Jeez, you're so educated and talented," one of them said, "and now you want to go to the Netherlands as a *babysitter*?"

My grandfather was particularly anxious. I totally understood how they felt, but my determination was strong and I would not be put off by their doubts and worries. I regretted that I had not heard about this opportunity when I was in my early twenties.

I planned to enjoy my one-year au pairing in the Netherlands. Then I would move to the next country, and work as an *au pair* again. I'd do a year in Denmark, followed by another in Norway. At the end of it all, I would be 29 years old. And I'd most likely be without a boyfriend. In a moment of doubt, I wondered if I'd end up as a spinster, old and alone. Instead of regretting my age, however, I focused on the opportunities and experiences I would soon be getting. Positive thinking gave me more energy.

The thought occurred to me: *I am not wasting my six-year relationship with Fendy. I'll count it as a life lesson.*

To learn and gain something, we need to invest our time, money and energy, don't we?

CHAPTER 4 - Embrace your UNIQUENESS and your PURPOSE

"Walk away from the 97% crowd. Don't use their excuses. Take charge of your own life." – Jim Rohn.

(Little me in the dress)

We all have differences in a world that values similarity. Fitting in means suppressing who you are and what you love the most but you will lose your opportunity to connect deeply with yourself – to live, to shine and to offer your unique talents to our society.

I used to… Used to do my best to fit in. In the family, in the surrounding and society.

I never felt comfortable…

Every time my big family had family meeting, I did not fit in as easy as my mother. She is extrovert, while I am a shy and introvert person. Same feeling when I tried to fit in the Chinese community or the Indonesian community. I was always the 'outsider' of the group. I knew I was different and trying to fit in was really devastating. I was unhappy. I did not like joining them spending their parent's money to hang out, to talk about how great their bags or their shirts were, or to listen to some accidental 'racist' joke because I was the minority. This broke my heart because I wanted to fit in so badly. I finally realized I was wasting a lot of time and energy by struggling to fit in.

Here are some examples indicating that you are trying to fit in:

• Always seeking approval from others to feel valued
• Compete with others

- Look for friends or partners who can complement us and giving us self-worth
- Change ourselves to please others
- Did not agree and feel happy into something but you do it anyway because people tell you to do so or because that is normal in your environment
- Wasting so much time in a job you don't even love
- Keep ourselves small just so that others will not feel threatened
- Get jealous of others owning their uniqueness and then try and copy it

Does it sound familiar to you?

We need to understand, my friends, that we are a unique individual. We might have similar face one another but our personality and our character are different to each other. You have your own will which your loved one might not understand.

Don't waste so much time and energy trying to be someone you are not!

Go back to the time when I had only two choices: to get married or to pursue my dreams. I unlocked all the courage I had inside and I chose to pursue my dreams. I chose to be different. While almost all girlfriends of mine have chosen to settle down, get married and stay at home (some of them who live in the big cities, however, they chose to keep their job), I chose to start my life over again. Leaving my comfortable life and went abroad. My family and friends thought I was totally crazy and out of my mind.

What will happen if I did not have the courage to take control of my own life and pursue my dreams? I would be a 'happy' house mom, with enough money to live a luxury life. But, do you think my life will be fulfilled? Money will not fulfil you.

In my culture, most of the parents will encourage their daughters to get married in their early twenty, and somewhere between twenty-five and twenty-eight for the male. My grandparents, my parents, my brother, my aunts got married around those age as well. But if I had listened to my family, my friends, my neighbours, my society, I will not be the person who write this inspirational story for you, who inspire many people and who help them to pursue their dreams. I have no regret at all at that time that I have chosen different path than a 'normal' lady in my age.

Look, you don't need to use different type of extreme clothes to be different...

Being different is showing the way you express yourself. Being different means you listen to yourself and even if it's not a common thing for you and in your surroundings, just do it, just do whatever you believe in. For example, I know a lot of successful entrepreneurs who did not have a supportive environment in the beginning when they started, when they were just about to open their mouth and about to share their ideas to be entrepreneurs.

Once you embrace your uniqueness, you can connect all the dots. Find the thread through a person, a tool, a task, a concept, an advantage and an opportunity. Connecting the dots will make your bigger picture clearer. Connecting the dots will sharpen your perception and approach to get closer to your dream or goals.

I quoted Steve Jobs' commencement speech at Stanford University in 2005 - six years before people would hang on every word out of grief. Standing before the nation's next generation of innovators was the genius who never graduated from college. He told the story of how he came to connect the dots of his past and went on to revolutionize technology.

"Of course, It was impossible to connect the dots looking forward when I was in college. But it was very clear looking backwards ten years later. Again, you can't connect the dots looking forward. You can only

connect them looking backwards. So you have to trust
that the dots will somehow connect in your future. You
have to trust in something - your gut, destiny, life, karma
whatever - because believing that the dots will connect
down the road will give you the confidence to follow
your heart, even when it leads you off the well-worn
path. And that will make all the difference."

Well, in my case, I actually connect the dots
from the past and the 'future'. Since I was a child, I
already pictured myself travelling abroad (even at that
time I knew that based on my situation it would not
happen). Every time I see a movie, I always imagined I
was there and I planted it in my mind. You have to
believe first before it happens and when you have the
courage to go for it, you will get it!

We might face the struggle to make sense of the
dots of our past. It's completely normal because when
your head is full of things, sometimes it's quite difficult
to see something clear. Sometimes you just get it when
you are not even thinking of connecting them. Just keep
going on and work on it. It's about understanding,
observing and listening.

To remind all of us, we were born as a winner.
You are a winner, even before you were born. Don't
believe it? Think again! There could have been hundred
million others who could have been in your place if they

were part of the lucky shot that got you conceived in the first place. You were the one to pop from your mother's womb for a reason.

When you wake up every morning, tell yourself that you are great and you can achieve everything you want! The only one who can prove you right or wrong is you, not others nor your circumstances.

HOW TO EMBRACE YOUR UNIQUENESS

1. Know who you are
2. Leverage and work with what you've got
3. Stand tall and be proud

CHAPTER 5 - How You Change Is How You Succeed

Dreams don't come true. Visions do!

"Uggh, this country is cold!"

The Netherlands was the coldest place I had ever been in. The atmosphere had a sharp bite to it and I was always cold, even in the summer. Dutch people would be at the beach in bikinis and swimming trunks while I accompanied my host family to the beach wearing a jacket. How embarrassing was that!

I enjoyed my role as an au pair. My host family loved me and "my baby" was so cute. Being with her almost every day endeared me to her. My days were full but I also had a lot of free time. While other au pairs went to the café or pub regularly (some of them loved to hang out, while others were on the hunt for a local boyfriend) I spent my free time as a solo traveller and participant in religious events.

Sometimes I got negative comments from some of them because I didn't join them as a group. But it was nothing personal. I wasn't into pubs, nor was I looking for a local boyfriend. Although going to church on my own in the Netherlands was a little boring, and I was mostly the only young person there, I still preferred doing this.

One by one, my *au pair* friends attracted local boyfriends, while I continued to make friends with non-

Asian *au pairs*, and Dutch people as well. But I had no romantic interest in European men. After all, my dream now was to marry a Korean! So I invented a Livia "mantra" that I used every time I met a man for the first time: "Please do not expect anything from me, I'm a conservative Catholic."

My host family laughed every time they heard me say it.

I was (and still am) proud of my track record! I went to ten countries and dozens of cities within the space of a year. I spent almost all my money on travel. And instead of just passing through the country by train, I actually visited all the cities and immersed myself in the culture. I was an active couch surfer. While I was crazy enough to trust the people in that organization, I never had a bad experience. All the experiences I had were brilliant, and more than money could account for.

(Austria & Slovakia)

(France)

One of my most unforgettable experiences was a visit to Prague.

Later, I joined a male couch surfer who was going to another city within the Czech Republic. When I think back now, I cannot believe I did it. He invited me to go to his villa in the middle of nowhere; the road was filled with twists and turns; and now I can't even recall the name of the place. But I got this nice picture below.

I was so crazy to have accepted that invitation! He gave me a nice big room in his villa, but to be honest, when I got there, I was really afraid.

What if something bad happens? I wondered.

There was nothing I could do to save myself because the villa was located on the outskirts of the city and it was a quiet place and with few neighbours. Of course, I did use my "mantra," and could only trust in God's protection. Throughout those three days, all we did was travel and walk around, soaking in the beauty of nature. It turned out to be a remarkable experience. But I would never go to a place like that if I had no contacts.

Access is important.

Anybody can watch a John Travolta movie. But personal access to him is much more powerful!

My experiences were invaluable. You get to a point in life when you realize that money doesn't bring experience; it is experience that brings money. I was fortunate to have been able to travel alone and stay safe. God was always with me and protected me. Yes, indeed!

(France)

Once I was walking around in Marseille (France), I met a man who offered to help me take pictures as there were no smartphones at that time. I agreed and afterwards we chatted. He followed me everywhere I went. We kept on chatting and he even paid my metro tickets, after a lot of argument between us. He insisted on paying despite my vehement objections, He treated me to a meal, too. This was the second time I felt afraid from hanging out with a stranger.

What if he is a bad person? O my God, what do I do? I wondered, and made myself even more anxious. But nothing happened. In the end, I thanked him very much for the day and we exchanged email addresses. He asked for nothing more.

Wow! How extraordinary is God! He sent two different kinds of people into my life. Some were to share good times with. Others were to give me a bad time. Both sets of people helped me in their different ways. The second group enabled me to grow stronger and tougher.

I was in the middle of my twelve-month contract as an *au pair* when I fell in love with a friend. He was a local and I met him in the Netherlands. He was all I wanted in a man, except for the fact that he was not

Korean. But I had outgrown my childhood and teenage fantasies by then and my soul recognized this man as my soulmate. I had a lot going on, however, and we decided to remain friends without take our relationship to the next level. I had deep feelings for him but I still wanted to continue my dream. I wanted to travel and be free. I wanted to be able to fly wherever the wind took me. I wanted to experience more cultural differences and to have the satisfaction of meeting all the challenges by myself. Those were the values that would distinguish me from others.

Unfortunately, with every reason I gave myself about why a relationship with him could not work out, my feelings grew stronger, and so did his. He told me he wanted me to start a family with him. However, after twelve months I went back to Indonesia. I thought about it deeply and finally decided to commit to our relationship. I made up my mind to live in the Netherlands as his wife.

Dear reader, you might be wondering how I could do such a thing! How was it that I could have had a six-year relationship before but never felt ready to commit? And now here I was, ready to commit within twelve months! Well, I can't explain it either. All I know is that I had a stronger feeling within those twelve months than I had ever had during my six years with

Fendy. I knew he could "handle" me and I chose to follow my heart. The heart wants what it wants, and only a strong man can handle a strong woman.

I went back to Netherlands and married the love of my life.

Soon, however, reality set in. I faced a lot of problems in the first year of our marriage. I came to realize that love was not enough. There were many obstacles that had to be faced, the biggest of which was unemployment. That really bothered me. I was jealous that my other Indonesian friends could get jobs. At least they had their own money and could make friends within their work environment. They had fun, while I didn't have a job.

It was not that my husband never gave me money. I had a good life and could buy everything I wanted because my husband gave me his bank ATM card. But I was not cut out for that sort of life. I was not the kind of person who could easily use my partner's money to have fun, buy fancy clothes or splurge in a restaurant. I wanted to have some money of my own. I wanted to be able to help my husband with the little things and not add to his worries.

Other problems were the language and cultural barriers. I overcame difficulties in the language by learning and improving my Dutch. It was not a big deal because I could learn Dutch at a good local college. The teachers and the school environment forced me to speak in Dutch. In the beginning, it was uncomfortable since some of the people in the class already spoke Dutch well. But I knew that the fastest way to learn a language was to try to speak it and that's what I did. Moreover, no one understood other languages. If I wanted to communicate, I had to learn their language.

Cultural barriers bothered me for a long time, as a conservative Indonesian lady. Living in the Netherlands as a permanent resident turned out to be totally different from living there as a short-term immigrant. In addition, my character as an Indonesian and as a person was (and is still) strong. So I hid at home. I tried to save my husband's money by avoiding unnecessary shopping. I hardly ever met friends as it was bound to cost money. Having a tea in a café would cost me at least two euros in the Netherlands, while that same amount in Indonesia would buy a meal in a good restaurant. Then there was the cost of the transportation to meet friends. I calculated everything. I had to because I wanted to go back to Indonesia every year and that would cost a lot of money. So the only time I left the house was to go to school. My free time was spent baking, cooking, and applying for jobs.

I also contemplated building a business, but no matter how much I thought about it, I couldn't come up with a feasible plan. I lacked confidence because of my limitations in the language and because I didn't know enough about the rules, the people and the culture. Meanwhile I became absorbed in my cooking and baking hobby.

I decided to start an online shop for wedding gowns, but failed simply because I lacked the will to continue. I went as far as creating a site and a marketing plans before I stopped.

Then I started providing services to the *au pair* industry. This time I at least made contacts with suppliers and customers, and could tell my story from experience, having been an *au pair* myself. I managed to get several clients, but a few months later the official rules for au paring changed. The Netherlands began to accept only those au pairs who came from a registered bureau and fulfilled some other conditions. However, instead of taking the necessary steps to make my business "official," I quit because I was not confident enough in Dutch to deal with all bureaucracy involved. So another initiative failed.

Based on all these disappointments, I was beginning to feel that maybe business was not for me. I had two choices left: either I could become a full-time mother or I could continue to study. I decided to plan for a child, and to look for a school.

I did the necessary homework and found a school that trained doctors' assistants. It was exciting to have something to do after being idle for so long. But then that I discovered something that made me happier than I ever thought possible. I found out I was pregnant.

My husband and I were over the moon! I thought things through and decided not to go to the school after all. I wanted to be a full-time mom, totally dedicated to my little family.

I enjoyed my pregnancy and my husband's banking career began to boom at this time as well. His team expanded and he was promoted to head of department. He had to travel around the world as the leader of an international team, and I joined him on many of his travels. Together we enjoyed life and I was happy. This time around, I was glad to be unemployed. Any boss I had would have been unimpressed if I'd taken a vacation every month.

I started to meet other mothers in the neighbourhood and to become more open to the culture. There was beauty in diversification. I didn't agree with everything in my new culture but I took what was best from my old one and merged them into something amazing.

Pregnancy and childbirth were among the best times of my life. Yes, I often felt tired, but at least I was busy and didn't have time to envy others. I didn't even have time to think about my sorry situation of being alone in another country with nothing to do. (Actually, I wasn't totally alone, but I was in my own for at least 40 hours a week.)

When I was pregnant, my husband actually began to ask himself what he wanted in life. We talked a lot about this and brainstormed together. He wanted to start a business of his own, but each time we discussed, it we almost always concluded that would "think about it again later." Was it fear that inhibited us? We had a good life, good money and he had a great job. What more could we want?

Meanwhile, I started to make money from my baking hobby. I catered for my friends too, and received many positive reviews. My customers loved my food, and I thrived on their compliments. It was still a home food business and I planned to open a small restaurant as well. But fear held me back. I guess I was afraid to fail.

My husband still went to seminars occasionally. One day, when our baby was around eighteen months old, he came home and told me, "We're going to South Africa, honey!"

"What? Why? When?"

"For seminars! And we're going in two weeks!"

"Are you crazy?" I couldn't believe what I was hearing.

Yet, we were on Safari, Africa, few days after the seminars.

After attending a couple of seminars, he felt confident enough to start his own Cyber Security business. He resigned from his job as a VP, and a few days later we got a call from a head hunter, offering him a full-time job. It was a top position in a bank in Switzerland. I found this exciting and asked him to think again. Couldn't he postpone building his business while gaining two or three years of life experience in Switzerland?

Now as I recall that moment, I can't help laughing at myself. It was ridiculous of me to give advice like that. Since reading Robert Kiyosaki's book as a university student, I had always believed that having one's own business was better than working as an employee. But somehow, when it came to the crunch, I was scared to venture out.

Perhaps, once again, I had stayed too long in my comfort zone. Or perhaps the opportunity to be the vice-president of a bank was too good to pass up. Was I simply afraid to fail or was it just that we'd be needing a lot money for start-up capital? I certainly didn't want to fail, especially as we had been living the good life for so long.

My husband was really determined, however, and all I could do was say yes and support him. Despite my fears, one thing was certain: his success, as well as our child's success, were mine.

After attending some seminars, my husband decided to be coached by an international business coach. He believed his company would be big and successful, and I was totally with him. I understood the future he envisioned for us, and I wanted to give him all the support I could. I caught the vision and volunteered to work in our business. We needed to make money in the beginning and I did not expect to take a wage from it. I worked part time and I learned.

After a couple months, the business expanded, and he needed more people. So he asked me to join him officially in running the company. Somehow, I believed I could do it, although I knew zilch about running a business. My background was in International Relations, and political science certainly not business administration.

Sir Richard Branson once said, "If someone offers you an amazing opportunity and you're not sure you can do it, say YES. Then learn how to do it later."

This was my chance! We had to grow together. I didn't want my husband to be stuck in his position and making no progress. We had to either grow or die.

Along with my determination, I also believed I had a lot to offer. Not that I knew exactly what it was, but I needed to find out.

My home catering business stopped as I did nothing to take it to the next level. I didn't do any marketing because the idea of running a professional business scared me. I was afraid to invest money in it because I was afraid of failing.

During the first year of running our IT company, I multi-tasked a lot. I was the personal assistant, and the second accountant. We had hired a certified public accountant, but I deputized for him to avoid any mistakes with the tax reporting. I was the manager, customer service person, debt collector, marketer and human resource consultant. I learned everything there was to learn in several fields, including IT and cybersecurity.

When I talked about cybersecurity, people's eyes glazed over. But I kept digging for knowledge about the industry and about building a business.

For the first two years, we spent almost all the money we made from our business on attending seminars and coaching sessions. My husband would say we were investing the money in learning. Sometimes I didn't agree with his decision, but with time, I too became addicted to self-education.

In 2015 we travelled abroad to learn and to network. We met our existing customers, potential customers and potential business partners. We always brought our child along, and would often explain to him why we did things.

"Mommy and daddy need to learn, love."

Taking our son along cost money and effort. We had to buy an extra ticket for the flight, and pay for the day-care or nanny in the hotel. I felt guilty about letting my child stay at different day-cares with foreign languages and foreign environments. Every two months it would be a new day-care in a different place. The first and second times were the worst. Every time I picked him up, he looked unhappy. That made me sad too, and I wished my family lived closer.

Short time sacrifice for long term results.

I tried to remind myself every time.

Luckily, after the second stint, the third, fourth and subsequent ones were easier. He was happy to stay in day-care in the USA. Soon he was used to it, and no longer cried when I picked him up at the end of the day.

I was relieved but still felt a little guilty. Moreover, going abroad so often was getting too much for me. I was feeling weary. I told my husband a few times that I would like to skip all business trips the following year and stay at home more.

I wanted to give up, yet I couldn't give up. It was not an option. I still had my responsibilities in our IT company. I had to help make my husband's business successful.

I could not forget a question from my coach: "Do you want your child to be successful?"

"Of course, I do!"

"Then you have to show him. Teach by example. That's how children learn!"

I started to think: *I provide my family with homemade healthy food. I support them with whatever they need and whatever I need to do. I have taught my child about positivity and life lessons since he was very small. My husband and I have shown him positivity and integrity. I take good care of the house. I have such a sweet and easy-to-manage child.*

As I reflected, I couldn't help but be proud. I was now successful as an immigrant, as a wife and as a mother, and it felt good. Yet I still missed something...

I wanted my child to be successful at something he loved doing. I wanted him to feel contented, fulfilled, and passionate about helping people. Since I wanted to be his example, I needed to be successful in business also, as myself, not as a part of my husband. I wanted him to see me climbing the stairs to success. If I was to build a legacy for him, I needed to push myself harder than I had ever imagined.

Success and wealth are products of process. Being unsuccessful and poor is also a process. A child who grows up in a successfully family will live around that process and adopt it in their own lives later on. It will be their standard. You are the key to your child's success. Be an example. Help and support them.

I realized I was not cut out for talking and networking. My husband and I actually complemented each other well, since he liked to talk with people while I preferred to write. It was a convenient separation of roles, but I knew I wouldn't grow if I kept hiding behind him.

We kept going to positive seminars and workshops, and as the year of 2015 ended, I committed to making 2016 my best year.

In January 2016, we were in Fort Myers, Florida, attending a workshop. The other participants were high-profile business leaders, compared to whom I felt small and invisible. One of our assignments was to pitch to an American billionaire as to why he should help or coach us. I wrote something for our pitch (as always, I wrote and he spoke) but this time he didn't feel my pitch was good enough, and he produced one himself. He was clearly nervous, which meant that despite his best efforts, nobody understood him. His pitch had too many technical terms.

During a short break, I plucked up courage and begged my coach, Damien, to give my husband another chance to pitch to the billionaire, because I strongly believed that he could do better. He agreed.

What happened after that was a big surprise!

After the break, my coach went to the middle of the circle and told the group there was one more person who was going to give a speech and… *it was me!*

In shock, I could only mumble to myself, *O my God!*

I had not prepared any speech, and I had not spoken in front of a group since presenting my university thesis more than twelve years earlier. I'd never needed to speak in public because I always stayed safely behind my husband.

The words of Richard Branson came back to my mind:

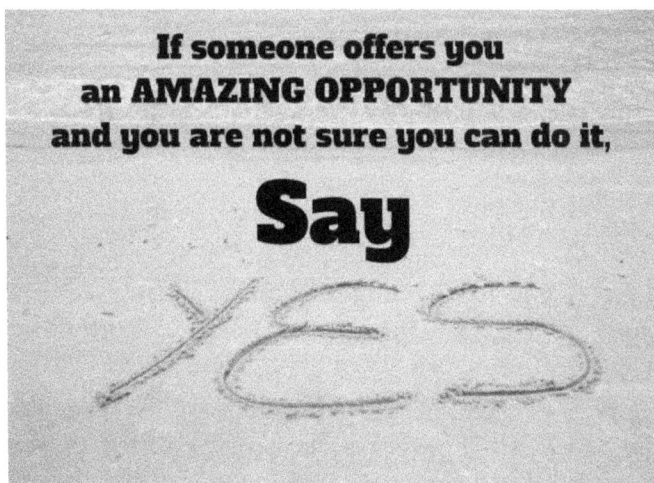

If someone offers you an AMAZING OPPORTUNITY and you are not sure you can do it,

Say

YES

Then learn how to do it later!

- Sir Richard Branson -

So this was my chance!

I stood up, trembling. My nerves were jangling and my heart was pounding so hard I thought it might burst out of my chest. Another coach came from his quick break and asked me, "What are you doing here in the middle of the group? We are done with the pitching!"

I was quite relieved. *Great, I don't need to speak!*

I wanted to hurry back to my seat, ready to listen again, but my coach, Damien, stood up for me. "No, I want to listen her".

The billionaire said, "Give her a chance!"

O my God, I thought, panic-stricken. *Please save me from this room! Make me disappear!*

I had asked God for the impossible. Now that I think about it, it was a request more suited to Harry Potter.

My knees were weak, but I was forced to stand firm.

I opened my mouth and began to speak. I could not see the eyes of the billionaire. Nor could I see those of my coach and the rest of the group. I still trembled, and my hands were ice-cold. I forced my voice to come out of my mouth and hey! I did my speech and finished it! But my mind was still paralyzed from the fear of the public speaking. Unfortunately, I could not digest all the feedback, but it was surprisingly positive. I hoped the writers were not lying! Well, at least they'd understood my non-technical pitch.

Afterwards, my coach Damien said to me, "Liv, you can inspire people!"

"Can I?" I didn't have time to pursue this, but I could never forget his words.

In the end I got an "award" too, for inspiring others who were afraid to speak. After they saw me do it, some stood up and gave a pitch as well.

See that? If I can do it, YOU can too!

I was so glad I did it. I was not the best pitcher but I'd inspired other people to conquer their fear.

My coach asked, "How can you teach your child to be brave and not to fear anything, while you yourself are afraid?"

True, I was afraid, especially of public speaking. In order to be a complete success, I had to conquer my fear of talking in public.

At one of the events I listened to Nick Vujicic, a most inspirational speaker, He had no limbs, and yet he could swim, surf, type and do many of the things I, a normal, healthy person, couldn't. I was so ashamed. I only had to open my lips, to speak. That was it. What was my excuse?

FEAR is the biggest disability of all.

Fear will paralyze you more than being in the wheelchair.

Nick Vujicic

It was true. Fear paralysed us! I would rather to do the things I fear than sitting in a wheelchair.

I decided to start doing new things, and take on challenges I once feared. As I started to come out of my shell, I grew tremendously in business and as a person. One day, I listened to Peng Joon, he is an international speaker and a successful businessman from Malaysia, he inspired me so much. I started planning my own business, I wanted to help more people.

In the meantime, our IT business grew rapidly. We implemented what we had learned, and we kept learning. Our team expanded and we delegated more jobs to our team members. We had more clients and prospects—more revenue and more profits. Basically, everything was much better. I realized more and more things. And I needed to, because now we were involved in massive projects.

One of the things I realized was that being the least successful person in the group, at a seminar or workshop, forced me to become better at business and as a person.

You are who you spend time with.

Please note that I was not competing with anyone, or trying to compare myself with others. I was only competing with myself—trying to be better today than I was yesterday.

2016 was my best year. I still can't believe that in one year I could do so much. I was transformed. Who could have imagined that a small town girl like me would ever met and trained by High Profile Figures, such people as George Ross (Trump's right hand man for 42 years), John Travolta, Vanilla Ice, Dr. Nido Qubein, 50 cents, Robert and Kim Kiyosaki, Randy Zuckerberg, Calvin Klein and JT Foxx.

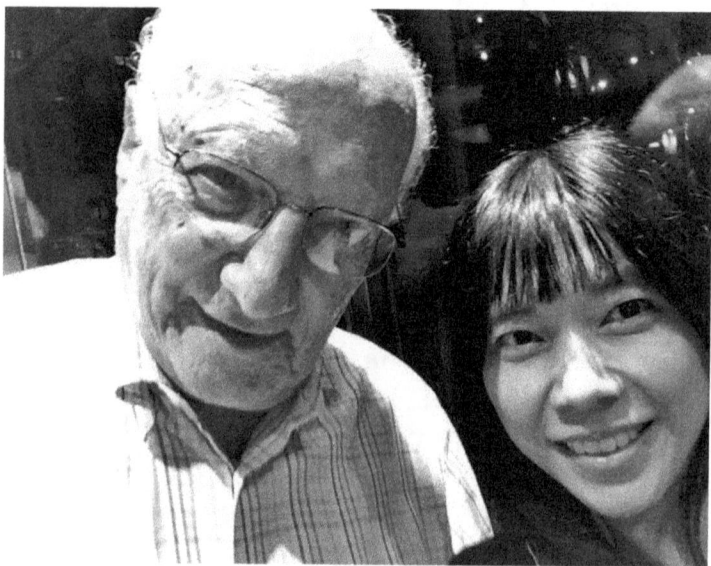

(selfie with George Ross)

Guess what…?

2017 is even better! I am proudly say that I am an international speaker. Helping people changing life by default into life by design is the reason why I travel internationally to speak.

In the end, I learned that dreams didn't come true. Visions did! I had envisioned my whole life since I was a little kid and my life decisions were actually congruent with my vision.

Based on this, I now want to help people to be the best version of themselves that they can be. I want to be the person who believes in you, who believes you can make a difference in your life, your family's life and the world. It takes only one person, one opportunity and one deal to change your life.

I want to be the person who climbs the stairs with you, helping you to achieve fulfilment in your life.

If I could do it, you can too!

I suggest you to visit www.LiviaLiyanto.com or www.EmpowerMeLivia.com to get to know me better.

Or simply scan the QR code below with your smartphone.

CHAPTER 6 - Elevate Your Passion Into Success

I started to change my mindset and my attitude. I spent a massive amount of money to learn.

We could buy a luxury real estate from the amount spent on our education, you would not believe. Yet, we prefer education to be our primary expense.

"If you think education is expensive, try ignorance."

If you have found your passion and, here is a summary of to elevate your passion and power into success:

1. Go to positive seminars or workshops

Do the research. Learn from someone who are already successful, who has done what you want to do.

If you don't know yet what do you want to do, that's fine too. By going to the different kinds of seminars, you will find out what do you want to do. Just keep moving and keep doing! The most important thing is to continue to educate yourself, because education will empower you. I'm talking here about specialized education.

I personally use a platform where I can learn and keep educated from successful speakers as Tony Robbins, Robert Kiyosaki, Blair Singer, T Harv Eker, Nick Vujicic etc. Simply by accessing it via my mobile phone. The platform is made by the biggest event producer in this world where they bring some of the biggest name on the stage. If you are interested to know, send an email to: gift@EmpowerMeLivia.com and put the text "platform" as subject and I will send you the tutorial how you can enter this platform. You can play around and see if this is something for you. If you want to use this platform, or not, it's your own choice. By being member of this platform, you can access some of the complimentary seminars, inspirations junctions for free and redeem any workshop. In this platform, not only you can keep educated, connect with people who have the right mindset and connect with some of the speakers, coaches and mentors, but you can make money as well, only if you choose to. Once again, if you choose to do it. I am passing the information just in case you need this.

I conduct workshops, mastermind, boot camp and speaking on seminars as well. You can follow my Facebook page where I post regularly and will keep you up to date to my events all around the world. Please scan this code to go directly to my Facebook page and to interact with me.

https://www.facebook.com/LiviaLiyanto/

Or scan this QR code right now with either your smartphone or tablet. You will be taken to my Facebook Page instantly.

2. **Find your mentor & coach**

"I suspect a lot of us wouldn't be where we are without mentors" – Sir Richard Branson

Whether you have a full-time job, are unemployed, are a housewife or even a business man/woman, you need to find a mentor & coach! Choose someone who is already successful, who has done everything you want to do or have. Not someone who learn to be a mentor or a coach but someone who has a business, who has done the business, who is a real businessman/woman. Which one you prefer, a doctor by certification but never perform a surgery or a person who perform thousands of surgeries already. Or a doctor who perform thousands surgery already?

Many of you might have many friends who are a mentor or coach already but based on my experiences in years, your family and your friends can not be your mentor or your coach. Believe me, I tried to mentor/coach my friends and my family but it doesn't work because they don't listen well. Your advice become subjective because they are close to you. My mentors and coaches told me since the beginning that I had to have a paid mentor & coach. I'm happy I listened to them!

"I am just a housewife…"

Don't be discouraged just because you are a housewife! Housewives are fantastic! You have a lot of hidden talents and passion (you are the manager, director, accountant of the house, look at how many talents you have!) Use it to pursue your hidden dreams! You are absolutely in the right place! Instead of spending your free time in front of the TV, please use the time to learn. Read books by successful authors and sharpen your mind.

David Beckham loved football as a youngster. He had a coach who sharpened and trained him until he became the David Beckham we all know and love. He had coach before he was famous, not after.

You need to have a mentor and or coach to be successful, so start looking for one *now!* In recent years, I have come to learn that even rich and successful people still have mentors and coaches in their lives.

Then the next most important thing is to *be coachable*. Since nobody knows it all, be ready to learn.

These are the biggest differences between a mentor and a coach, in my opinion.

	COACH	MENTOR
Goal	Short Term	Long Term
Orientation	Task-oriented	Relationship-oriented
Purpose	Performance-driven	Development-driven

3. Surround yourself with successful and positive people

When you are in your comfort zone, you will not grow. Leave your shell and discover that you are not alone. If it feels scary, it's always felt that way. Don't give up or retreat! Keep doing it. Having done this myself, I know exactly how it feels. But I don't let my fear define me anymore. That's now in the past. Remember, I forced myself to be surrounded by successful people, and in the end, I realized this had enabled me to grow.

Because I went to a Dutch language class which forced me to speak in Dutch, my ability to speak this language increased significantly. You don't develop, if you don't have the right people around who push you to be better.

4. Have an accountability partner or positive community

This partner could be your coach. But if you don't talk to your coach daily or weekly, find other people who can keep you accountable. It could be your husband or a club made up of positive people. At the end of the day, we are much more likely to take action if someone is taking note and tracking our goals.

5. **Apply what you learn. JUST DO IT!**

If we do not apply our knowledge, it will be worthless. It is better to take action and to make mistakes than to do nothing. Once we take an action, we learn from it and become better for it. And most important—by taking action we build self-confidence!

Check here to see what people and my mentees say about say about me:

https://empowermelivia.com/what-people-say-about-livia/

You can also download a free app (QR Code Reader) to help your work easier, just scan this code and it will give you instant access to the site.

CHAPTER 7 - Where Do You Go from Here

"A year from now you may wish you had started today."

Congratulations for making it this far. You have now been exposed to an inspirational story which could bring you ideas and concepts. But no matter how good your ideas are, just being exposed to them is not enough. You must also do something with them. Ideas are nothing more than ideas until they are put into action.

Now you have the knowledge, idea and encouragement – now it's up to you to put those into action. Once you take an action, you will learn from it and become better. And most important—by taking action you build your self-confidence!

My friends, instant results will come to you once you have the right mindset and the right tool. But if you don't have the right mindset yet, it could take a long time. So my suggestion is to learn about mindset and have the right mindset first.

I will teach more and deeper about mindset through my process, because I believe it is very critical for you to have the right mindset in order to attract the success you deserve, either in health, physics or financial.

If you decided to embrace my LIV system and process, please send your application to info@EmpowerMeLivia.com. I have different courses for you to choose, depends on your needs. If you are accepted, you will be a part of my community, a group of positive and successful people. I will guide you step by steps and I will not let you fail. It will save you 10+ years learning of process. You are welcome to learn from my mistakes and be empowered, you'll potentially find a happier future, making more money, having the lifestyle you desire and having more time with your family.

What is LIV system?

L – Learn2Lead

I – Implement2Improve

V – Value2Profit

After learning, you have to implement the things you have learned. Because no matter how good your ideas are, just being exposed to them is not enough. You must also do something with them. Ideas are nothing more than ideas until they are put into action. Implement it! Once you implement, you will learn from it and become better. The best part is that I will be mentoring you to implement your ideas. If it's not enough, the other students of mine will keep you accountable as well so you will not stop implementing until you become successful. And most important—by taking action you build your self-confidence! And then, you can share your value and experiences to help other people and to monetize. You will shine.

I have other courses in positioning, marketing and branding as well if you need it.

"Self-improvement is a necessity, not an option."

EPILOGUE

Thank you for reading my book. This is just the beginning. I'm learning every day and striving to be a better person. I have coaches and mentors who support me and push me to improve.

Success doesn't happen overnight. It's the sum of small efforts repeated day in and day out.

However, as I look back, I can proudly say that this journey is an instant success. For some people, it may take them more than twenty years of their life to achieve success, some maybe less. I am happy that I have been investing a lot of money on my mentors and coaches, they saved me 10 to 20 years' process of learning.

It is possible to have INSTANT RESULTS. For example, many people are searching for happiness. But you can have INSTANT HAPPINESS within seconds. How? Simply watch a baby giggles, enjoy smelling your favourite home cooked dish being prepared by your mom, sing your heart out loud in the car, call your friends and chat endlessly or crack and listen to jokes.

I teach my mentees how to achieve instant results by doing specific habits which lead them to attain their goals. Anything is possible, my friends!

Instant results will come to you once you have the right mindset and the right tool. That's the reason why I will talk more and deeper about mindset in my course, because it is very important for you to have the right mindset in order to attract your success and wealth, either in health, physics or financial.

I'm passionate about helping others to make progress in their lives. Especially women. Yes, I'm speaking to *you*, strong women! Because I am a woman myself. But I train men as well. My process and my system are easy to follow for both men and women.

For you ladies, we need to understand our power. We have always multiplied and enlarged whatever men have given to us.

When a man gives us his *smile*, we give him our *heart*.
When he gives us *groceries,* we give him a *meal*.
When he gives us a *house*, we give him a *home*.
When he gives us *sperm*, we give him a *baby*.

How powerful is that?

We have so much to give. Let's discover what we are capable of and feel that incredible power. Let's not stay in the shadows any longer, although I know from experience that they are a comfortable place to hang out in. I was there once, and when I started to step out, it was far from easy. But let's keep pushing through, and when we find our passion we will be wonderfully fulfilled.

I know many people out there who became coaches because they were trained at school. I've experienced transformation and gotten the breakthrough. I walk my talk. I run the businesses myself. I've known the ups and downs of the business and life, so I can feel what you feel. Then give you the right tools and strategies.

Finally, someone who can understand you, feel your pain, somebody you can relate to. Because many people don't understand you as I do. I will empower you and open the door to the prosperity, you'll have all the tools you need to make a positive difference in your life.

Yes, it can be scary to suddenly do something you are not comfortable with, but luckily you don't have to jump from an airplane (literally)! You just need to do an extra one percent every day and do it consistently. After 365 days, you will start next year with an extra

365 percent! It has to start now. If it's not now, then when? If it's not me, then who? If it's not you then who? When is the right time to make this year your best year ever? Now. When is the right time to become happier? Now. When is the right time to make extra money? Now.

Remember, if I can do this, and Nick Vujicic can do it, you can too. I am no different than you. Stop doubting!

Let me express my biggest thank you to the following people:

- My husband and my child for their unstinting support, and to my big family.

- My ex-boyfriend Fendy who set me free so I could reach for the stars.

- My first mentor, Joko. I'm sorry about all the times I bothered you so much and for the times I forgot to say thank you.

- My coach, Damien for believing in me and gave me the first chance of speaking.

- All the mentors and coaches I'm working with now. I love you!

- My friends in Indonesia. I miss you guys a lot! Ivan, Emma, Maya, Icha, Ronald: thank you always being open and for giving me a lift during our time at school.

- My team.

- Julie Belding, thank you for your help!

- Joyce and Leonardo who helped me in the final process.

- Everyone who has helped me to make this book possible. Your gifts will be cherished for years to come. Know that it is never too late to continue growing in all aspects of your life.

- Those few people who bullied me when I was a kid.

Being bullied as a child taught me many lessons. I am proud that I can share this story to inspire others to let it go and move on. You are in control of your future. Do not let anyone else define your future!

- Finally, thanks to you! Yes, YOU! I love you!

I would personally love to hear about your experience after you have read this book and taken the actions I've suggested. Please review your comments on Amazon because your comments might help others to potentially change their life.

You can get weekly inspirational and empowerment video or how-to video by subscribing to my Youtube channel. Click here to see more video's from me.

I'm looking forward to connect with you via my Youtube channel or my Facebook page.

https://www.facebook.com/LiviaLiyanto/

In case you did not have the chance to scan the code earlier, here is the code…

Can't wait to see you soon!

Lots of love,

Livia Liyanto

As promised, these are my gift to you, two tickets for you and your guest to my live event. I cannot guarantee your seat, so please make sure to register in advance. You may also bring another guests, your spouse, partner, or your family if I still have room.

I wish you can transform your life as I did. I believe you will benefit more from my live event. Nothing can substitute live experience.

Enter your email on this page:
https://empowermelivia.com/instantresults
and we will send you the information about my upcoming events.
Or simply scan this code: